Put Beginning Readers on the Right Track with
ALL ABOARD READING™

The All Aboard Reading series is especially for beginning readers. Written by noted authors and illustrated in full color, these are books that children really and truly *want* to read—books to excite their imagination, tickle their funny bone, expand their interests, and support their feelings. With three different reading levels, All Aboard Reading lets you choose which books are most appropriate for your children and their growing abilities.

Level 1—for Preschool through First Grade Children
Level 1 books have very few lines per page, very large type, easy words, lots of repetition, and pictures with visual "cues" to help children figure out the words on the page.

Level 2—for First Grade to Third Grade Children
Level 2 books are printed in slightly smaller type than Level 1 books. The stories are more complex but there is still lots of repetition in the text and many pictures. The sentences are quite simple and are broken up into short lines to make reading easier.

Level 3—for Second through Third Grade Children
Level 3 books have considerably longer texts, use harder words and more complicated sentences.

All Aboard for happy reading!

In memory of Doris

Copyright © 1992 by Nicki Weiss. All rights reserved. Published by Grosset & Dunlap, Inc., which is a member of The Putnam & Grosset Group, New York. ALL ABOARD READING is a trademark of The Putnam & Grosset Group. GROSSET & DUNLAP is a trademark of Grosset & Dunlap, Inc. Published simultaneously in Canada. Printed in the U.S.A.

Library of Congress Cataloging-in-Publication Data
Weiss, Nicki. The first night of Hanukkah / by Nicki Weiss. p. cm.—(All aboard reading)
Summary: As a family gets ready to celebrate Hanukkah, a young girl learns how the holiday began. [1. Hanukkah—Fiction.] I. Title. II. Series. PZ7.W448145Fi
1992 [E]—dc20 91-32147   CIP   AC

ISBN 0-448-40389-7 (GB)   A B C D E F G H I J
ISBN 0-448-40387-0 (pbk.)   B C D E F G H I J

ALL
ABOARD
READING™
Level 2
Grades 1–3

THE FIRST NIGHT OF
HANUKKAH

By Nicki Weiss

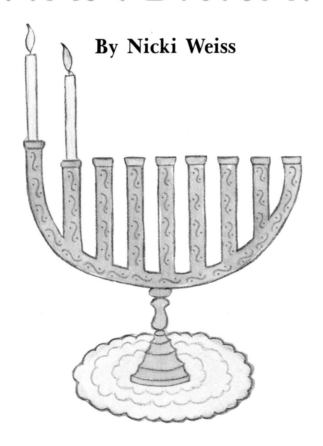

Grosset & Dunlap • New York

It was the first night of Hanukkah.

Everyone was getting ready.

Grandma was in the kitchen.

Dad was helping make potato pancakes.

Mom was setting the table.

And Molly was helping Uncle Dan polish the menorah.

Uncle Dan said, "When I was your age,
I helped my mother polish this menorah.

"And now you are helping me.

It is a tradition that we are passing on.

That is how it was.

And how it still is."

Molly wanted to know

what else he remembered.

"I always lit the candles,"

Uncle Dan said.

"But first my mother

would tell me

the story of Hanukkah."

Uncle Dan put Molly on his lap.

"Would you tell me the story?"

asked Molly.

"Sure," said Uncle Dan.

A long, long time ago there was a king.

His name was Antiochus.

(You say it like this—An-TIE-uh-kuss.)

King Antiochus ruled over

all the people of Israel.

But the king had a hard heart.

He made a law.

Everyone in the land

had to pray to all his gods.

Now the Jews of Israel

prayed to only one God.

They would not obey the king's law.

"We will keep on praying

to our one God," they said.

"We will not pray to many gods."

You can imagine.

This made King Antiochus very mad.

He told the Jews,

"If I catch you praying to your one God,

you will be killed!"

Then the king sent his army

to the Jewish Temple in Jerusalem.

This was the most important place

for Jews to pray.

The soldiers broke

all the holy things in the Temple.

They put a statue

of one of their gods inside.

And so the Jews

could not pray there anymore.

But this did not stop the Jews.

There was a brave man named Mattathias.

(You say it like this—MAT-uh-TY-yass.)

He lived in the village of Modin

near Jerusalem.

Mattathias and his five sons

still prayed to one God.

Other Jews heard about Mattathias's family.

From far and near they came to join them.

They learned about Jewish ways.

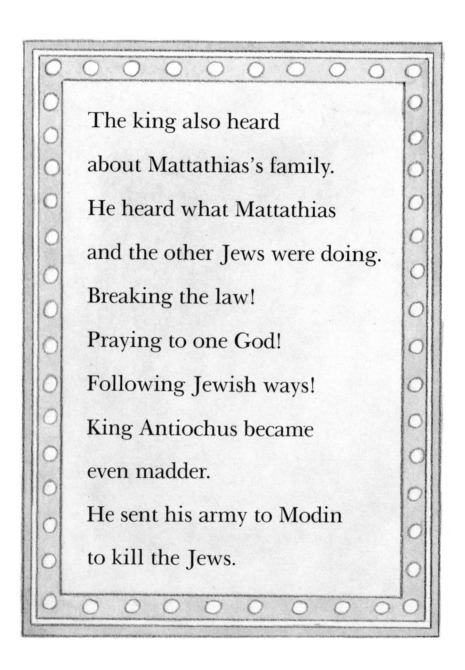

The king also heard

about Mattathias's family.

He heard what Mattathias

and the other Jews were doing.

Breaking the law!

Praying to one God!

Following Jewish ways!

King Antiochus became

even madder.

He sent his army to Modin

to kill the Jews.

But the Jews of Modin were ready to fight.

They were ready to protect

their right to be Jews.

So a long struggle began.

On and on it went.

For three years

the Jews fought the king's army.

Mattathias died.

But his son Judah Maccabee

became their leader.

Judah was a great fighter.

Under him the Jews fought

long and hard.

The king's army was big.

Even so, it could not win.

The Maccabees just would <u>not</u> give up.

In the end the king's men gave up and left.

What a great day!

Judah led everyone to Jerusalem.

Now they would take back their Temple!

They would make it beautiful again.

They would make it holy once more.

All the Jews would be able

to pray there again.

Everyone went to work.

They cleaned . . .

and polished.

They got rid of the statue
of the king's god.

They made a new altar.

At last the Temple was ready to open again.

Special prayers were said.

Then it was time to

light the great menorah.

But there was only a small jar

of holy oil.

It was all the Jews could find.

The jar held enough oil

for just one day.

Still the lights
kept on burning
for eight days!

"It was a miracle!" Uncle Dan said.

"And since that time Jews have celebrated

the holiday of Hanukkah.

"We use a special Hanukkah menorah.

It has a place for eight candles.

There is also a place

for the shammash.

That is the candle

that lights the others.

We light one candle on the

first night of Hanukkah.

We light two on the second.

And so on.

"On the last night eight candles are lit.

Eight nights to remind us

of the miracle of the oil.

And to remind us of brave

Judah Maccabee and the Jews.

"And that's the story of Hanukkah,"

Uncle Dan said.

Molly got down from his lap.

"Just in time!" Grandma said.

She put a plate of potato pancakes
on the table.

Dad put down
bowls of applesauce
and sour cream.

Mom said, "Now let's light the menorah."

Uncle Dan put one candle
in the menorah.

He lit the shammash.

He handed it
to Molly.

46

Molly lit the first candle

of the first night of Hanukkah.

She said a prayer.

Just like Uncle Dan had done

when he was her age.

A tradition being passed down.

How it was.

How it still is.

How it will always be.